THE NEGRO LEAGUES

CELEBRATING BASEBALL'S UNSUNG HEROES

Millbrook Press
A division of Lerner Publishing Group, Inc.
241 First Avenue North
Minneapolis, MN 55401 USA

For reading levels and more information, look up this title at www.lernerbooks.com.

Main body text set in Adobe Garamond Pro Regular 14/19.
Typeface provided by Adobe Systems.

Library of Congress Cataloging-in-Publication Data

Names: Doeden, Matt, author.
Title: The Negro Leagues / Matt Doeden.
Description: Minneapolis : Millbrook Press, [2016] | Series: Spectacular
   Sports | Includes bibliographical references and index. | Audience: Ages:
   10–18. | Audience: Grades: 4 to 6.
Identifiers: LCCN 2016017079 (print) | LCCN 2016032857 (ebook) |
   ISBN 9781512427530 (lb : alk. paper) | ISBN 9781512428452 (eb pdf)
Subjects: LCSH: Negro leagues—History—Juvenile literature. | Baseball
   teams—United States—History—Juvenile literature.
Classification: LCC GV875.A1 D63 2016 (print) | LCC GV875.A1
   (ebook) | DDC 796.357/640973—dc23

LC record available at https://lccn.loc.gov/2016017079

Manufactured in the United States of America
1-41486-23349-7/22/2016

CONTENTS

Many great players of the Negro Leagues, such as Buck Leonard *(left)* of the Homestead Grays, are not well known to modern fans because they were not allowed to play Major League Baseball.

INTRODUCTION

BASEBALL'S UNTOLD STORY

Imagine Major League Baseball (MLB) without home run champion Hank Aaron. No over-the-shoulder, game-saving catches from the great Willie Mays. No towering home runs off the bats of Ken Griffey Jr. or Reggie Jackson. No diving stops by Frank Robinson. No blazing Bob Gibson fastballs. No Rickey Henderson racing around the base paths.

To a baseball fan, it's almost unthinkable. Baseball, more than any other major American sport, treasures its history. The modern game was built on the shoulders of these legendary players and others. Imagining baseball without them feels a little like imagining the game without third base. And yet, just 70 years ago—less than a lifetime—you wouldn't have had to imagine. Then many of the game's greatest players—those who didn't have white skin—weren't allowed to play in the big leagues.

But that doesn't mean they didn't play. For decades, baseball's Negro Leagues offered fans a thrilling alternative to Major League Baseball. The history of black baseball is steeped in tall tales and legend. The lines between fact and fiction are often blurred, the truth lost to history. Most Negro League stars remain unrecognizable to all but die-hard baseball history buffs. Yet for students of America's pastime, the true story of baseball can never be complete without the tales of these heroes.

Bud Fowler (*back row, middle*) poses for a photo with his teammates in 1885. Teams such as this one, which was based in Keokuk, Iowa, often had a mix of white and black players.

1 THE SEGREGATION

OF PROFESSIONAL BASEBALL

Baseball's modern era began in 1901. That year the American League emerged, joining the National League as one of the game's two major professional leagues. It's the point from which most of the game's all-time records are kept. Many modern fans pore over every statistic and bit of data that comes after 1901, while all but disregarding that which came before. Yet pro baseball didn't begin in 1901. For decades before the advent of the modern era, the game was taking shape both on and off the field. And that's where the story of baseball's 60-year segregation begins.

After America's Civil War (1861–1865), the earliest seeds of professional baseball began to sprout. And while racism was rampant—overtly in the South, less openly in the North—some early teams featured black and white players competing side by side.

Not all early pro leagues embraced integrated baseball. In 1867 the National Association of Base Ball Players voted to exclude any team that had black players. Their reasoning was particularly telling of racial views of the period. The association claimed that by including blacks, "there would in all probability be division of feeling, whereas by excluding them no injury could result to anybody."

PIONEERS

Two men—Moses Fleetwood Walker and Bud Fowler—helped blaze the path for black players at the highest ranks of pro baseball.

MOSES FLEETWOOD WALKER

Moses Fleetwood Walker, regarded by most historians as the first African American to play major organized baseball, was born in 1856 in Mount Pleasant, Ohio. In 1883 he signed with the minor-league Toledo Blue Stockings. While with Toledo, Walker ran into the Chicago White Stockings and outspoken racist Cap Anson. Anson threatened to cancel the game if Walker played. But the Blue Stockings didn't budge, and Anson eventually gave up on his demand.

In 1884 Toledo joined the American Association, a major league. Walker's major-league debut was a disaster. He made at least four errors in the game and didn't record a hit. He suffered a season-ending injury in July, and Toledo folded after the season. In total, Walker played 42 major-league games, batting .263.

Walker's baseball career ended in 1889. The business owner, publisher, and inventor remained an advocate for civil rights until his death in 1924.

BUD FOWLER

Bud Fowler grew up in Cooperstown, New York, the future home of the National Baseball Hall of Fame. Fowler spent about 25 seasons playing pro ball. He gained his first real measure of fame in 1872 when he took the mound and defeated Boston's National League team, 2–1.

Fowler understood that the game's highest profile position was pitcher and that it would be coveted by his white teammates. So, to improve his chances of playing with the top pro teams, he switched to second base. Fowler was one of the great players of the time. Yet no National League team would pick him up. According to an 1885 article in the popular sports newspaper the *Sporting Life*, "The poor fellow's skin is against him. . . . Those who know, say there is no better second baseman in the country."

After his playing career, Fowler helped found the Page Fence Giants, which enjoyed a brief existence as the class of black baseball. Yet for all his success, Fowler battled poverty and illness after his baseball career ended. He died in 1913, penniless and buried in an unmarked grave.

Despite such logic and despite abuse from fellow players and fans, some leagues allowed black players to take the field alongside white players. Early black legends such as Bud Fowler, Moses Fleetwood Walker, and Welday Wilberforce Walker made their marks alongside white teammates. By 1887 many fans, especially in the northeastern United States, were used to watching a sport that was at least partially integrated.

But that was about to change.

A LINE IN THE SAND

After the Civil War, the North and South struggled to rebuild a nation that had been ripped apart by conflict. Part of the mending of their shattered union was the Compromise of 1877. The agreement effectively ended the openly hostile relationship that had existed between the two sides since the end of the war. As a result, the white-dominated Democratic Party took control of the southern states. Among the measures these politicians enacted were laws mandating public separation between blacks and whites. Ten years later, these Jim Crow laws, as they were called, would change the shape of pro baseball.

It all started with a single game. Cap Anson, a future Hall of Famer, had been one of the most popular players in the early pro game. By 1887 Anson was the manager of the Chicago White Stockings (the present-day Chicago Cubs). On July 14, 1887, his team was scheduled to play an exhibition game against the integrated

Cap Anson played pro baseball for 27 years, mostly for the Chicago White Stockings. Anson opposed integrated baseball.

Newark Little Giants. When Newark's George Stovey—a talented black pitcher who had played in Canada—took the field, Anson reportedly shouted racial slurs, demanding that Stovey leave.

It wasn't the first such incident for Anson. He was, even by the standards of the day, an outspoken racist. Four years earlier, he'd said his team wouldn't play against an integrated team, though they eventually took the field. This time, Anson wasn't going to back down. The Little Giants—in need of the money from the game—relented. Stovey was removed from the game. He watched from the dugout alongside catcher Moses Fleetwood Walker.

At the moment, the events of July 14, 1887, may not have seemed important. But that very day, the International League voted to avoid such situations in the future. The league agreed that no further contracts would be offered to black players. The league cited Jim Crow laws in the South, arguing that including blacks would lead to clashes with legalized segregation. Soon the National League and the American Association followed suit. By the 1890s, the brief era of integrated pro baseball was effectively over. Blacks and later other minorities were barred from the big leagues.

Some have dubbed Cap Anson the father of segregated baseball. And while his positions may seem indefensible to modern observers, some historians note that Anson really had no power to ban

Since African Americans weren't offered contracts by major-league teams in the 1890s, they formed teams of all-black players.

STANDING OPPOSED

The segregation of baseball was widely accepted at the time. Yet some called out the injustice. Among them was the *Newark Sunday Call*, which published the following in 1887:

> If anywhere in the world the social barriers are broken down it is on the ball field. There . . . the best man is he who plays best. Even men of churlish disposition and coarse hues are tolerated on the field. In view of these facts the objection to colored men is ridiculous.

Meanwhile, Welday Wilberforce Walker, a black player in the Ohio State League (and brother to Moses Fleetwood Walker), issued a plea for the ban to be repealed in 1888. He wrote,

> The law is a disgrace to the present age . . . and casts derision at the laws of Ohio—the voice of the people—that say all men are equal. . . . There should be some broader cause—such as lack of ability, behavior and intelligence—for barring a player, rather than his color.

blacks from the game. Those decisions came from team owners and, to a lesser degree, from white fans whose ticket sales endorsed the practice.

THE BARNSTORMING ERA

Integrated pro baseball at the highest levels was ending. But even before the International League's 1887 decision, baseball was largely segregated. Players like Stovey and Walker were the exception rather than the rule. A few black players had played on integrated teams before 1887, but the vast majority played on all-black teams.

An 1887 attempt to start an all-black league, the National Colored Base Ball League, fell flat, not lasting even a single season because of low attendance. Rather, it was another model that found success. Black teams of the era, lacking home stadiums, took to the road. They were barnstormers, traveling the country, taking on all comers, from local clubs to major-league teams. While the major leagues barred black players, teams could play against black players in exhibition games. The players earned their pay by taking a portion of the ticket sales.

One team, the Cuban Giants, set the standard for early barnstorming teams. In truth, there was nothing Cuban about the team, which originated in New York in 1885. Yet the players, most of whom were working-class black men, passed themselves off as foreigners, who were generally treated with more respect than African Americans. Some Giants players went so far as to speak nonsense to one another on the field, hoping it made them sound like Spanish-speaking Cubans to the English-speaking fans.

The Giants were a hit and not just because of their gimmick. The team could play with anybody, and it often challenged and defeated big-league

This portrait of a barnstorming team was taken around 1885.

Fans in Worcester, Massachusetts, line a hill to watch the Cuban Giants take on the local team in 1916.

opponents. For a few years, the Giants were the standard for all-black baseball. Their success didn't go unnoticed. In 1888 the *Indianapolis Freeman*, a black newspaper, said, "The Cuban Giants . . . are virtual champions of the world. The St. Louis Browns, Detroits, and Chicagos, afflicted with Negrophobia [fear of black people] and unable to bear the odium [disrepute] of being beaten by colored men, refused to accept the challenge."

TERMS OF THE TIME

The words "Negro" and "colored" were commonly used to refer to African Americans in the late 1800s and into the 1900s. In modern times, both terms are considered offensive except when used in a historical context.

The Chicago American Giants, shown here in 1914, were one of many teams hoping to benefit from the success and name recognition of the Cuban Giants.

Their success inspired more than a few imitators. From the Cuban X-Giants to the Columbia Giants, the Brooklyn Royal Giants, and the Genuine Cuban Giants, plenty of teams looked to cash in on the team's brand identity. For more than 30 years, it seemed half of the top barnstorming teams bore the name Giants.

THE GOLDEN AGE OF BARNSTORMING

The Cuban Giants had helped usher in a new, somewhat profitable age of black baseball. Of all the imitators the team inspired, perhaps the most successful was the

Page Fence Giants. The team played for just four seasons, but they were four seasons unlike any before or since.

Successful barnstorming teams had learned that entertainment and spectacle were every bit as important to ticket sales as the play on the field. A baseball game in the late 1800s was a social affair, as much about the gathering as it was about the balls and strikes. The Michigan-based Page Fence Giants, organized in part by the legendary Bud Fowler, understood this well. The Giants brought the sideshows that the fans loved. The players would ride into town on a parade of bicycles. They performed tumbling routines. Players even sang songs to the crowd between innings.

None of that diminished their play on the field. The magical four-year run actually started with a huge thud. The Giants lost their first game, 26–1. But it didn't take long for the team to become the class of black baseball. In 1896 they

BLURRED LINES

For six decades, Major League Baseball was mostly a white man's game. Some American Indians were allowed to play. Blacks weren't welcome. But the color line blurred when it came to players of Latino descent. Generally, light-skinned Latinos were accepted into the big leagues. Among them was Cincinnati Reds pitcher Adolfo Luque *(right)*, who won 27 games in 1923 and was, perhaps, the first big-league Latino star. Meanwhile, dark-skinned Latinos were barred. Many, such as catcher Martín Dihigo, played in the Negro Leagues.

challenged the Cuban Giants to a 15-game series. Page Fence won, 10 games to five, staking their claim as the best black team in the land. A year later, the team went 125–12, a record that included a shocking 82-game winning streak. Despite their great success, the team disbanded in 1898. Many of the players moved on to the newly formed Columbia Giants.

The barnstorming era stretched into the 1900s. Major League Baseball had entered its modern era, and in 1903, the first World Series was held. But black baseball was thriving as well. The Kansas City Monarchs, Chicago American Giants, Indianapolis ABCs, and St. Louis Giants were among the most successful clubs of the period. While the product on the field certainly rivaled that of Major League Baseball, the barnstorming teams also maintained the tradition of sideshow and spectacle. Players weren't just players. They were entertainers, promoters, and even ticket salesmen. Their games—often doubleheaders and triple-headers—became social events. As the popularity of the games spread, profits grew. And so, although black baseball teams had formed in response to segregation and racial mistrust, they became some of the most successful black-owned American businesses of the time.

RUBE FOSTER'S VISION

One of the most popular black players of the barnstorming era was pitcher Rube Foster. Foster, though, dreamed of a day when players of all races would share the big-league diamond together.

By the late 1910s, Foster had come to a realization. He believed that the very aspects that had made barnstorming successful and profitable—the sideshows and spectacle—were also holding back the cause of integrating Major League Baseball. Foster reasoned that no matter how many times black teams beat white teams in exhibition games, many fans and opponents would regard the black players as showmen first, and baseball players second. Foster believed that to be

A great player during the barnstorming era, Rube Foster went on to become a team manager, an owner, and a league executive.

taken seriously, black players needed to abandon the antics and focus only on baseball. It was an idea that could never work in a barnstorming setting, where the quality of competition was wildly varied and even the rules could change from game to game. Foster proposed creating an all-black major league.

Foster's idea wasn't an easy sell. Several all-black leagues had formed over the past decades, and none had lasted even a season. When Foster approached owners of some of the biggest barnstorming teams with the idea of a National Negro League (NNL), they resisted, fearing yet another failure. But Foster was persistent and persuasive. On February 14, 1920, he gathered owners of several top teams for a meeting in Kansas City, Missouri. And he finally got his wish. Eight owners banded together to form the NNL. Some—including Foster—wanted to exclude the Kansas City Monarchs, owned by white businessman J. L. Wilkinson. But Foster, knowing that the fate of the league hung in the balance, ultimately changed his mind. Wilkinson's reputation with black players was positive. He was liked and respected, and the other NNL owners accepted the Monarchs, white ownership and all.

This photo of J. L. Wilkinson's All Nations team was shot in Kansas City, Missouri, around 1915. The barnstorming team had white and black players as well as American Indians, Latinos, and Asians.

Foster understood the pitfalls of the new league. Because teams didn't follow a common set of rules during the barnstorming era, players had simply gone to the highest-bidding team. Fearing one or two dominant teams that would destroy the NNL's balance and cause fans to lose interest, Foster prohibited teams from raiding one another's rosters. He further demanded that the owners shift players to balance rosters. Foster also wanted the teams' barnstorming to end. When all eight teams managed to find stadiums to play in, the NNL was ready to begin. Foster's dream was about to become reality.

2 PLAY BALL!

The 1920 season was a time of massive change in professional baseball. With the rise of sluggers such as Babe Ruth of the New York Yankees, an infusion of offense gave Major League Baseball an enormous boost in popularity. Yet while the headlines belonged to Ruth, another change—one not found on the front pages of national newspapers—would also reshape the game. The newly formed National Negro League was about to change black baseball forever.

A NEW ERA

On May 2, 1920, the NNL opened its first season with eight teams centered in the Midwest. The Indianapolis ABCs beat the Chicago Giants in the league's first game, 4–2. (The Chicago Giants and Rube Foster's Chicago American Giants were the two Chicago-based NNL teams.) Just getting the NNL off its feet had been a monumental challenge. None of the NNL teams owned their own stadium. They had to lease stadiums from white teams in their area. That made scheduling a nightmare. If a game was canceled because of bad weather, it was almost impossible to make it up. And sometimes, teams would just skip league games to play a better-paying barnstorming game. By season's end, the final standings was a mess because teams had all played a different number of games. The 1920 pennant was awarded to Foster's Chicago American Giants.

Instability also plagued the NNL. The league as a whole was a moderate financial success. Yet not all the teams were able to match that success. After just two seasons, half of the original NNL teams were gone, replaced by new ones. High team turnover would be a problem for the NNL throughout its existence.

Despite these troubles, the play in the NNL met the standard Rube Foster had sought. With the barnstorming sideshows stripped away, the league provided a showcase for some of the best black ballplayers in the country. Despite Foster's

The Chicago American Giants were one of the NNL's best teams in the 1920s. The 1922 team, shown here, was managed by Rube Foster.

THE FATHER OF BLACK BASEBALL

Andrew "Rube" Foster *(right)* was a giant in baseball history even before his greatest accomplishment. Born in Calvert, Texas, in 1879, Foster quit school after the eighth grade. He ran away to play baseball. Foster's barnstorming days made him a mythic figure. Legend has it that he taught Hall of Famer Christy Mathewson how to throw a screwball.

Late in his career, Foster shifted his attention to managing. Once again, he was among the best. His fellow managers called him a master planner and an excellent judge of talent. He was hard on his players but also generous.

In time Foster took over ownership of the Chicago-based American Giants, one of the most successful black teams in the Midwest. He used his influence as an owner to establish the NNL, and he controlled the league's operations from 1920 to 1926, all while remaining owner and manager of the American Giants. Foster was well respected as the league's boss, though sometimes he was criticized for favoring his own team. Some opposing teams noted that the Giants seemed to have more home games than anyone else.

By 1926 Foster's family had grown concerned about his increasingly erratic behavior. He had become paranoid and spoke wildly. Foster's family placed him into an institution, citing mental illness. Foster died there in 1930. He was 51 years old.

POMPEZ   FOSTER

initial hope for balance throughout the NNL, the league was marked by dynasties. In 12 seasons from 1920 to 1931, only three teams won the league championship. The Chicago American Giants won it five times. The Kansas City Monarchs won four titles. And the St. Louis Stars claimed three.

THE COLORED WORLD SERIES

The success of the NNL inspired new leagues in other parts of the country. The Negro Southern League (NSL) also started in 1920, though many regarded it as a secondary league with lesser talent. The Knoxville Giants won the first NSL title.

The NNL's main rival was the Eastern Colored League (ECL), which began play in 1923. The ECL was centered in the nation's Northeast. While Foster had established rules preventing NNL teams from raiding one another's rosters, no such agreement existed between leagues. And so the ECL, which served larger fan bases and had deeper pockets, quickly poached much of the talent in the NNL by offering players more money. Eastern teams signed away future Hall of Famers such as Oscar Charleston, Biz Mackey, and Pop Lloyd. So many players flocked east that several NNL teams had to fold.

Tension between the rival leagues was high. But in 1924, they called an uneasy truce and announced that the two league champions would meet in a Colored World Series (also called the Negro World Series). The series pitted the ECL champion Hilldale Club against the NNL's Kansas City Monarchs.

Oscar Charleston

Biz Mackey

Pop Lloyd

The 1924 Kansas City Monarchs

The two teams played a 10-game series, which included games in Chicago, Kansas City, and Philadelphia—cities where black baseball was thriving. The Monarchs, led by a stellar pitching staff and a speedy outfield, were heavy favorites.

The drama-packed series didn't disappoint fans. In one pivotal game, Kansas City clung to a 2–1 lead. In the eighth inning, Hilldale loaded the bases with nobody out and the heart of the batting order coming to the plate. Yet not a single runner scored, and the Monarchs held on for the victory.

The series was deadlocked, 4–4–1, entering the 10th and final game. The drama began before the first pitch was even thrown. Kansas City pitcher José Méndez, suffering from an arm injury, was under doctor's orders not to pitch. But the hard-throwing righty took the mound anyway. He delivered a performance for the ages, dominating the Hilldale hitters. "For inning after inning," wrote sportswriter

José Méndez   Scrip Lee

Carl Beckwith, "[Méndez] kept the Easteners popping up or grounding out. Not a man reached second, and only four reached first. It is improbable that Méndez will ever pitch another such game."

Meanwhile, Hilldale pitcher Scrip Lee matched Méndez zero for zero. The game remained scoreless into the eighth. That's when Lee switched from his standard sidearm style of pitching to the traditional overhand style (possibly because of arm fatigue). The Monarch hitters, baffled by Lee up until then, began to see the ball more clearly, and they teed off. They scored five runs in the inning. It was more than enough. Their 5–0 victory gave Kansas City and the NNL the title.

The Colored World Series carried on for just four years. Hilldale avenged the loss the next season, beating Kansas City five games to one. It would be the ECL's only victory in the series. The Chicago American Giants won in both 1926 and 1927. The series ended abruptly when the ECL folded in 1928 because of disputes between owners, as well as disputes between owners and players.

THE DISAPPEARING BALL TRICK

The history of the Negro Leagues is rich with colorful and amazing tales, some more believable than others. Hitters belting 600-foot home runs. Outfielders sitting down with the tying run on base because they were so sure that ace pitcher Satchel Paige would strike out a batter. Base runners sprinting all the way to second base on a bunt before the ball was even fielded. Many of the tales are obvious fiction, but some actually appear to be true. Among the strangest such tales is of a 1930 game between the Homestead Grays *(below)* and the Kansas City Monarchs.

It was a night game (the Negro Leagues used artificial lighting years before MLB did). Pitchers Smokey Joe Williams of the Grays and Chet Brewer of the Monarchs were locked in an epic duel. Brewer, using an emery board to scuff up the ball and alter its flight, struck out 19 batters. The 45-year-old Williams, annoyed at his opponent's tactic, fought back. He spit tobacco juice all over the ball. The dark juice made the ball all but impossible for batters to see, allowing Williams to rack up a jaw-dropping 25 strikeouts. Modern baseball rules prohibit the use of emery boards and tobacco juice to gain an advantage on the mound, but no such rules existed in 1930.

The game finally ended when the Grays' Oscar Charleston drew a walk and was later driven in by Chaney White. White's game-winning hit was little more than a routine ground ball that deflected off of third base and into foul ground. But the ball was so dark from Williams's tobacco juice and the lighting in the stadium was so poor that the ball was hard to see. White scored the game-winning run as the Monarchs chased after the ball.

Homestead Grays of 1930
3-20-??
HARRISON
HOT SPRINGS
ARK

THE RISE OF THE EAST-WEST CLASSIC

The East-West Classic soon became the premier event of the season for fans of black professional baseball. "You'd get people from every city," said center fielder Gene Benson, who played in three Classics. Many modern-day players don't regard all-star games as very important. But that wasn't so in the 1930s. Then the prestige and paycheck that came with the game really mattered—especially to Negro League players, who made considerably less than their major-league counterparts.

"The East-West All-Star Game was a very serious event," according to baseball historian Larry Lester. "The major league All-Star Games were more of an exhibition, a showcase. In the Negro Leagues, it was just the opposite."

When it comes to ranking all-star games in baseball history, the 1934 East-West Classic can stake a strong claim as the greatest of all time. Unlike the first East-West Classic the year before, this game was a pitcher's duel. It was scoreless in the bottom of the fourth when the West's Mule Suttles laced a one-out triple. Red Parnell stepped to the plate. He drove a pitch from Harry Kincannon to shallow right field.

Players line up for a photo at the East-West Classic on August 26, 1934.

Suttles tagged up at third base as the East's Jimmie Crutchfield made the catch. Crutchfield fired it home to Josh Gibson, who tagged out the charging Suttles to end the inning and the rally.

The scoreless tie dragged on. The East managed a rally in the top of the eighth inning. Cool Papa Bell drew a leadoff walk and then stole second base. He remained at second base with two outs. His teammate Jud Wilson stood in the batter's box, facing a two-strike count. Willie Foster delivered the pitch. Wilson popped the ball into the air. The ball didn't go far. It dropped between the second baseman and the shortstop. Bell, running on contact, tore around third base to score the game's first and only run. Pitcher Satchel Paige held the West scoreless in the final two innings to seal the East's exciting 1–0 victory.

A year later, Suttles was at the center of another thrilling finish. The game was tied, 8–8, in the 11th inning. Slugger Josh Gibson, this time playing for the West, stepped to the plate. Gibson already had four hits on the day. Suttles, batting fifth, was hitless. With one out and a runner on second base, Suttles wanted a shot at redemption. He called pitcher Willie "Sug" Cornelius to come out of the dugout and kneel in the on-deck circle. Seeing what he thought to be an easy out on deck, the East's pitcher, Martín Dihigo, intentionally walked Gibson. Suttles then stepped to the plate instead of Cornelius and crushed a three-run homer into the stadium's upper deck.

If there had been any doubt, the 1934 and 1935 East-West Classics showed fans that black baseball was back, and it was better than ever.

Catchers take a beating behind home plate, so many catchers aren't good hitters. Josh Gibson managed to play catcher for 17 seasons and still mash the ball when he came to bat.

LOS DRAGONES

During the off-season in the United States, many baseball players headed south to play winter baseball. In nations such as Mexico and Cuba,

black players were treated as equals. Jim Crow laws didn't apply there, and fans and reporters showered them with attention—a welcome change for players more used to abuse than respect. Black, white, and Latino players shared the diamond, rode the same buses, and stayed in the same hotels. Some black players, tired of the racial climate in the United States, simply stayed.

Winter ball wasn't a well-paid affair. But that changed, briefly, in 1937. Rafael Trujillo was the dictator of the Dominican Republic. He had changed the name of the nation's capital to Trujillo. The dictator dreamed that having the world's greatest baseball team play in the city bearing his name would boost his popularity with the Dominican people. So Trujillo hired pitcher Satchel Paige to raid the Negro Leagues and assemble a super team—Los Dragones *(above)*. The dictator gave Paige a budget unlike anything ever seen in Negro League play, much less in winter ball.

Paige didn't let Trujillo down. The Dragones roster was full of Negro League all-stars. Paige, Cool Papa Bell, Josh Gibson, and Sam Bankhead were among the headliners. The team won the Dominican League title. Yet Trujillo wasn't satisfied. He had wanted to utterly crush all competition. Winning the title hadn't been good enough. So he disbanded Los Dragones—a team whose talent may have rivaled that of the powerful New York Yankees—the following year.

NEW LEAGUE, NEW DYNASTIES

The 1937 season saw the formation of the Negro American League (NAL), which debuted with seven teams from the South and Midwest. The best known was the Kansas City Monarchs. After the team's dominance in the first NNL, the Monarchs had returned to their barnstorming ways. Their return to league play marked the beginning of a second dynasty in Kansas City. The Monarchs were led by a stellar pitching staff that included Satchel Paige and Hilton Smith. They won the NAL's first title in 1937 (although it was disputed because the league's teams played an unequal number of games). They won four in a row from 1939 through 1942.

While the Monarchs ruled the NAL, the 1937 season also witnessed the rise of a new power in the NNL, the Homestead Grays. Home run hitters Josh Gibson and Buck Leonard powered the popular Grays to the NNL championship that season. It was the beginning of one of baseball's great dynasties, with the Grays winning nine straight NNL titles from 1937 to 1945.

Two of the Negro Leagues' biggest stars, Satchel Paige *(left)* and Josh Gibson *(right)*, led their teams to dynasties in the 1930s and 1940s.

3 COUNTDOWN
TO INTEGRATION

By the 1940s, political and social change was sweeping the world. World War II (1939–1945) had broken out in Europe, and the United States entered the fray in 1941. At home the civil rights movement was gaining steam, with blacks and other minorities demanding an end to Jim Crow laws and calling for equality. Baseball, in some ways a reflection of society, was about to change forever.

THE WAR YEARS

With the United States fighting World War II in Europe and Asia, countless thousands of young men went to war—men of all races, black and white alike. The nation's baseball talent was badly depleted. The Negro Leagues called on older stars such as Satchel Paige to lead the way while many of the younger players fought for their country.

Among the highlights of the 1941 season was the annual East-West Classic in Chicago. The talent-laden game attracted a crowd of more than 50,000 fans. According to Monte Irvin, who played in the game, "More than anything else, our games gave black Americans hope all across the country. . . . They said, 'If these ball players can succeed under these very difficult conditions, then maybe we can too.'"

The 1942 season marked the beginning of a new Negro World Series, pitting the NAL champion Kansas City Monarchs against the NNL's Homestead Grays. The series included a moment that has become a baseball legend. In game 2, the Monarchs led 2–0 in the sixth inning. The Grays loaded the bases. Josh Gibson, probably the best hitter in the game, stepped to the plate against the great Satchel Paige. It was a clash between the two biggest stars in the Negro Leagues. Paige won the battle, striking out Gibson on three pitches. Kansas City held on for the victory on their way to a four-game sweep of Homestead.

The Grays earned redemption in the 1943 series, this time facing the Birmingham Black Barons. Game 6—a 1–0, 11-inning classic won by Birmingham—sent the series to a deciding seventh game.

Birmingham led, 4–1, with two outs in the eighth inning. But the Grays took advantage of some timely hitting, as well as Birmingham errors, to score four runs in the inning and seize control. They tacked on two more in the ninth inning for an

The 1942 Homestead Grays

8–4 victory and the championship. Homestead repeated as champs in 1944. They lost to the Cleveland Buckeyes in 1945.

ROBINSON AND RICKEY

By the time World War II ended in victory for the United States and its allies in 1945, the social landscape in the country was changing dramatically. Blacks and whites had fought side by side in Europe and in the Pacific. As soldiers returned home, many wondered that if people of different races could fight and bleed and die together in defense of their country, why couldn't they share a baseball diamond?

Integration still faced major resistance, and not just from white MLB owners. During the war, the Negro Leagues had exploded in popularity. Profits for Negro League team owners were higher than ever, and baseball was one of the nation's most successful black-owned businesses. Negro League owners realized that integration would spell the end of the Negro Leagues and their profits, and many resisted it.

Branch Rickey believed that baseball should be integrated for moral reasons. He was also a savvy businessman who knew a good opportunity when he saw it.

Despite pressure from both sides, some people were determined that baseball's long segregation should end. Among them was Branch Rickey, general manager of MLB's Brooklyn Dodgers. Rickey was a pioneer, having invented baseball's farm system to develop young talent. He had a proven track record as a winner. Renowned in baseball as a bit of a cheapskate, Rickey didn't shy away from a fight.

By 1945 he was ready to change the game he loved one more time. Some have said his desire to break baseball's color barrier was a quest for social justice. Others think he simply wanted to profit from an untapped pool of talented players. Or perhaps it was a combination of the two. Regardless, Rickey set out to break the color barrier, a mutual agreement between teams and not an actual rule. He heavily scouted the Negro Leagues, searching for the perfect player. He wanted a man who could handle the pressures both on and off the field. In October 1945, Ricky found that man—Kansas City Monarchs infielder Jackie Robinson.

Jackie Robinson, shown here in 1945, was an infielder for the Kansas City Monarchs before signing with the Brooklyn Dodgers.

Robinson was a sweet-swinging, smooth-fielding speedster well suited to the MLB game. But what really set Robinson apart was his personality and background. He was cool, calm, and college-educated, with a military background. He had a history of standing up for his rights, having refused to sit in the back of a segregated bus while serving in the US Army. Robinson seemed the perfect candidate to endure the hardships that would come with breaking baseball's color barrier.

"[Robinson] knew what to do about pressure," explained future teammate Don Newcombe. "He knew how to handle pressure. He had [racial abuse] happen to him while he was in the military as a second lieutenant, how he was treated because of the blackness of his skin."

Rickey signed Robinson to a minor-league contract. In 1946 Robinson joined the Dodgers' top farm team, the Montreal Royals of the International League.

The 27-year-old quickly erased any doubts of whether he belonged. Robinson led the league with a .349 batting average and 40 stolen bases.

ROBINSON BREAKS THE BARRIER

One year later, on April 15, 1947, Robinson took the field as a Brooklyn Dodger, officially ending baseball's six decades of segregation. His reception was far from warm. He suffered taunts and threats from fans, opponents, and even teammates. Dodger fan-favorite Dixie Walker started a petition to have Robinson kicked off the team (the Dodgers soon traded Walker). A handful of team owners scrambled in an unsuccessful attempt to bar Robinson from the league. On a road trip to Philadelphia, Robinson was refused service at the team's hotel and taunted. Even Philadelphia manager Ben Chapman unleashed an infamous barrage of racial slurs toward Robinson. The abuse was intense and relentless. Robinson received piles of hate mail from all over the nation, as well as death threats.

Jackie Robinson posed for this photo just days before his debut with the Dodgers.

Yet Robinson remained stoic. His example off the field, as well as his success on it (he batted .297, stole 29 bases, was named National League Rookie of the Year, and finished fifth in National League Most Valuable Player voting) changed the way many fans thought about integrated baseball. Perhaps most important to MLB owners was his impact on attendance. Fans of all races flocked to games when

First baseman Jackie Robinson *(right)* poses with the rest of the Dodgers infield on April 15, 1947. Some of Robinson's teammates were unhappy about his presence.

the Dodgers came to town. For most owners, the promise of increased revenue was enough to overcome whatever racial biases they might have held. Rickey and Robinson had led the way, and others were quick to follow.

The color barrier was broken. Robinson's debut was hailed as a major civil rights victory. The major leagues would never be the same. But neither would the Negro Leagues. For good or bad, their time was quickly ending.

THE DEMISE OF THE NEGRO LEAGUES

Suddenly, doors once slammed shut on black players were opening. Cleveland Indians owner Bill Veeck had long advocated for integrating baseball.

He was one of the first to react once Robinson had broken the color barrier. Veeck signed outfielder Larry Doby, who debuted with the team on July 5, 1947, to become the American League's first black player.

The floodgates had opened. Major-league teams began scooping up the best talent the Negro Leagues had to offer. The draw for black ballplayers was clear. The pay was better, and the lights shined brighter. Those who left their Negro League teams included seasoned veterans, such as 42-year-old Satchel Paige, who signed with the Indians in 1948, as well as rising youngsters such as Willie Mays, who signed with the New York Giants two years later.

While integration was a cause for celebration for many, the exodus of players to the big leagues left a monumental talent gap. The Negro Leagues were doomed. The NNL disbanded in 1948. Several of its teams joined the NAL, the only remaining Negro League.

Baseball historians believe that the competition in the NAL remained about equal to MLB until about 1950. From then on, the NAL played at something like a semipro level (in which part-time players are paid small amounts), with many teams just barely scraping by financially. Records and statistics for the Negro Leagues had always been spotty at best. After integration, they became all but nonexistent as attention shifted to MLB. The NAL finally disbanded in 1960. It was the official end of an era. But realistically, Negro League baseball had been dead for more than a decade.

A few former NAL teams carried on after the league folded, barnstorming semipro clubs composed mainly of players who lacked big-league talent. The last of them was the Indianapolis Clowns, which finally disbanded around 1988. Baseball's final tie to the Negro Leagues was no more.

4 LEGENDARY PLAYERS

OF THE NEGRO LEAGUES

For most of their history, the Negro Leagues were virtually ignored by major newspapers. And while official scorekeepers carefully kept statistics for MLB games, statistics were messy or often nonexistent for Negro League games. Baseball historians simply don't have much hard data about many players and teams, especially those from early in Negro League history. This knowledge gap makes it hard for modern fans and historians to put the feats of Negro League players into context.

Modern fans must rely on oral history and stories of the Negro Leagues that have been recorded. The tales told by players and fans paint vivid pictures of these players and their games. But how can one know which stories really happened and which are tall tales? Which are exaggerated for effect, and which describe genuine amazing performances? Would Josh Gibson truly have outslugged Babe Ruth, as many who saw him play insist? Was Satchel Paige the greatest pitcher of his time, black or white? Was Cool Papa Bell a faster version of Ty Cobb? We'll never have definitive answers to those questions. But for many fans of the game, the mysteries and myths that surround the great players of the Negro Leagues are as appealing as the hard statistics used to measure their major-league counterparts.

COOL PAPA BELL

The pure speed of Cool Papa Bell is the stuff of legend, and there were no shortage of tall tales to describe it. Josh Gibson said that Bell was so fast that if he hit the light switch in his hotel room, he could be in bed before the bulb began to dim. According to Satchel Paige, "One time he hit a line drive right past my ear. I turned around and saw the ball hit him sliding into second."

James Thomas Bell was born May 17, 1903, in Starkville, Mississippi. At the age of 17, he moved to St. Louis to live with older brothers and attend high school. But instead of spending his days in a classroom, he spent them on a baseball diamond. Bell started out playing semipro ball as a pitcher. He signed with the NNL's St. Louis Stars in 1922. He earned the nickname Cool for his calm manner on the mound. In time, "Papa" was added, probably just to make the nickname roll off the tongue a little better.

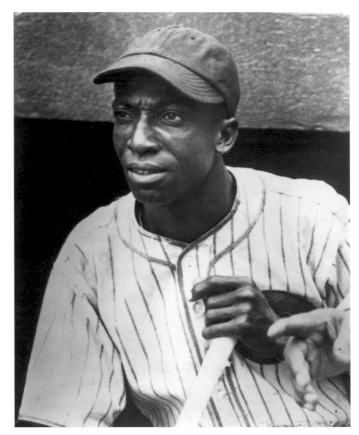

Cool Papa Bell

Starting around 1924, Bell shifted to center field, where his great speed could be better used. Bell was never a slugger, but he was an accomplished hitter who could

Cool Papa Bell slides into third base as a member of the Homestead Grays around 1944.

bunt with the best of them. Catcher Ted "Double Duty" Radcliffe noted that "if [Bell] bunts and it bounces twice, put [the ball] in your pocket [because you won't be able to throw him out]."

Bell was the centerpiece of St. Louis teams that won NNL titles in 1928, 1930, and 1931. Later in his career, he played for the Pittsburgh Crawfords. The team was the powerhouse of the Negro Leagues at that time, featuring five players who would go on to baseball's Hall of Fame. In the 1940s, Bell played for the Homestead Grays. With the Grays, he won championships in 1943 and 1944. Later in his career, he was a manager and scout for the St. Louis Browns.

Bell was elected to the Hall of Fame in 1974. He died in 1991.

BUCK LEONARD

Buck Leonard was the complete package. A sure-handed, strong-armed first baseman, Leonard's smooth stroke made him one of the great contact hitters of his day. Long compared to contemporary big leaguer Lou Gehrig, Leonard could do it all. "Trying to sneak a fastball past him was like trying to sneak a sunrise past a rooster," noted fellow star Monte Irvin.

Born September 8, 1907, in Rocky Mount, North Carolina, Walter Fenner Leonard's nickname, Buck, came from a younger brother. Leonard developed an early fascination with baseball. As a child, he'd sneak to a segregated field to peer through a fence and watch white players. His hometown of Rocky Mount didn't offer a high school education to African Americans, so Leonard had to find a job after eighth grade. He started working at a railroad shop and eventually played semipro baseball, where he attracted the attention of the Homestead Grays.

Most Negro League players moved from team to team, but Buck Leonard spent his entire career with the Homestead Grays.

Leonard made his Negro League debut in 1934 with the Grays. He would remain with the team for his entire 17-year career, the longest any player stayed with one Negro League team. Leonard was an anchor for the Grays. Fans and players called him one of the best pure hitters in the game. He posted a career batting average of .320. Beginning in 1942, he helped the Grays reach the Negro

World Series four straight times, winning it in 1943 and 1944. In 1948 Leonard and the Grays defeated Willie Mays and the Birmingham Black Barons in the final Negro World Series.

In 1952 the 45-year-old was offered a big-league contract. Leonard turned it down. "I knew I was over the hill," Leonard later explained. "I didn't try to fool myself."

Seven years later, at the age of 52, Leonard finally earned his high school diploma. He was elected to the Hall of Fame in 1972. He remained an advocate for civil rights until his death in 1997.

JOSH GIBSON

Perhaps no player in Negro League history inspires more awe and mystery than catcher Josh Gibson. He was called the greatest power hitter of his day. He belted an estimated 800 home runs in his career, while posting a career batting average over .350 (possibly as high as .384, depending on the source). Satchel Paige was blunt in his assessment of the slugger, saying, "He was the greatest hitter who ever lived."

Gibson didn't just hit home runs in bunches. He hit mammoth shots. His home runs dropped jaws. One of his home runs in Yankee Stadium was supposedly measured at 580 feet.

Josh Gibson sometimes played third base or left field in addition to catcher, but he was best known for the thunder in his bat.

According to a teammate, Gibson once hit a ball completely out of Yankee Stadium, over the third deck in left field. No other player in history ever hit a fair ball completely out of the stadium.

Gibson was born December 21, 1911, in Buena Vista, Georgia. His family moved to Pittsburgh when he was young. As a teenager, Gibson built a reputation playing semipro ball.

Gibson's Negro League debut sounds like a storybook. In 1930 he attended a game as a fan in Pittsburgh between the Homestead Grays and the Kansas City Monarchs. Homestead catcher Buck Ewing suffered an injury and was forced to leave the game. Manager Judy Johnson had heard Gibson was a powerful young slugger, and Johnson knew Gibson was in the stands. Johnson pulled the 18-year-old down from the stadium seats and put him into the game. Homestead signed Gibson to a contract the next day.

Through 17 seasons, Gibson spent time with the Grays, the Pittsburgh Crawfords, and with several teams in Latin America. He terrorized pitchers, hitting for both average and power. Meanwhile, he was a rock behind the plate, with a cannon for an arm that made any base runner think twice before attempting a steal.

According to player and manager Alonzo Boone, "Josh was a better power hitter than Babe Ruth, Ted Williams, or anybody else I've ever seen."

Satchel Paige, who knew Gibson as both an opponent and a teammate, described the nightmare of pitching to him: "You look for his weakness and while you're looking for it, he's liable to hit 45 home runs."

Gibson's personal life, however, was marred by tragedy. In 1930 his young wife, Helen, died during childbirth. In 1943 Gibson fell into a coma with a brain tumor. When he regained consciousness, his doctors recommend surgery. Gibson refused, fearing it would rob him of his intellect. Despite crippling headaches, Gibson returned to the diamond. He died of a stroke on January 20, 1947—just three months before Jackie Robinson broke the color barrier. Gibson was 35 years old. He was elected to the Hall of Fame in 1972.

POP LLOYD

Pop Lloyd in 1914

John Henry "Pop" Lloyd was a star before the Negro Leagues even started. A run-scoring machine and a brilliant shortstop, Lloyd made his name with barnstorming teams such as the Cuban X-Giants. Fans in the United States called him the black Honus Wagner, comparing his game to that of the Pittsburgh Pirate great. Wagner called the comparison to Lloyd an honor.

By the time the NNL came into existence, Lloyd was in his mid-30s. He served as a mentor to many of the younger players, a role that earned him his nickname, Pop. Lloyd was a player and a manager in the Negro Leagues. Even with the prime of his career behind him, he posted a career average of .337.

"Pop Lloyd was the greatest player, the greatest manager, the greatest teacher," said teammate Bill Yancey. "He had the ability and knowledge and, above all, patience. I did not know what baseball was until I played under him."

Lloyd continued on as a player through the 1932 season, when he was 48 years old. Even after he left the pro game, he spent time as a coach at the semipro and youth levels. He died in 1964 at the age of 79. Lloyd was inducted into the Hall of Fame in 1977.

TONI STONE

The Negro Leagues boasted something Major League Baseball still has not had—female players. Their inclusion was, to a large degree, a publicity stunt. Yet one of the women, Toni Stone *(below)*, proved that a woman could share the diamond with men and hold her own.

Marcenia Stone was born in St. Paul, Minnesota, in 1921. As a child, she got her nickname, Toni, because it sounded like "tomboy." By 1937 Stone was playing for a semipro team in St. Paul.

Stone appears to have played semipro ball on and off for the next 14 years. Then in 1953, the Indianapolis Clowns of the NAL offered her a contract. Stone jumped at the chance. In her first game, she stroked a single to drive in two runs. She played in 50 games that season, batting .243. According to Stone, the highlight of her career was getting a hit off of future Hall of Famer Satchel Paige. The claim, however, proves hard to verify. Baseball historians have found no evidence that she ever faced Paige.

"A woman has her dreams, too," Stone said in 1991. "When you finish high school, they tell a boy to go out and see the world. What do they tell a girl? They tell her to go next door and marry the boy that their families picked for her. It wasn't right. A woman can do many things." In 1993 Toni Stone was inducted into the International Women's Sports Hall of Fame.

OSCAR CHARLESTON

Oscar Charleston may have been the greatest player that casual baseball fans have never heard of. Baseball historian Bill James ranked Charleston as the fourth-best player in baseball history. It was a well-earned title. Charleston, known as much for his fiery temper as for his all-around brilliance on the field, could do it all. He was a speedster, a defensive wizard in the outfield, and one of the most reliable left-handed bats the game has ever seen. According to Hall of Fame first baseman Buck O'Neil, "He was like Ty Cobb, Babe Ruth, and Tris Speaker rolled into one."

Oscar Charleston began his career as an outfielder but later moved to first base.

Charleston was born in Indianapolis, Indiana, in 1896. As a child, he was a batboy for the Indianapolis ABCs. He joined the US Army at the age of 15 and served in the Philippines. Upon his discharge in 1915, Charleston returned to the ABCs, this time as a player.

Charleston was described as intense, with a fierce will to win. He never backed down from a challenge. One story tells that he ripped the mask from a member of the Ku Klux Klan (a hate group that targeted blacks) so he could confront the man.

But it was his actions on the field that made him famous. In 1921 Charleston led the NNL in doubles, triples, and home runs. Charleston was often on the move, from team to team and league to league. But wherever he went, he excelled.

In 1932 Charleston became a player-manager for the Pittsburgh Crawfords. He managed the team until 1937 and during that time had the best team in the Negro Leagues. Some regard the team as the greatest in Negro League history.

Charleston died in 1954, at the age of 57. He was elected to the Hall of Fame in 1976.

Ray Dandridge played some winter baseball in Cuba. This photo was taken in Havana in 1951.

RAY DANDRIDGE

Ray Dandridge is widely considered the greatest third basemen in Negro League history, despite playing only a handful of seasons in the United States. While an accomplished contact hitter, Dandridge's defense was his true calling card. "There simply never was a smoother functioning master at third base than Dandridge," said Cum Posey.

Dandridge was born August 13, 1913, in Richmond, Virginia. He was a natural athlete who excelled at almost any sport. But he soon zeroed in on baseball. In 1933, at the age of 19, he made his Negro League debut with the Detroit Stars. At first, Dandridge didn't seem destined for greatness. He batted a woeful .218 in his first season.

That all changed in 1934. Dandridge signed with the Newark Dodgers (later called the Eagles) and burst onto the scene. He batted a scalding .408 (which either led the league or was second, depending on the source). Dandridge was Newark's anchor in what fans called the million-dollar infield, but despite the team's talent, Newark could never get past powerhouses such as the Pittsburgh Crawfords and Homestead Grays.

In 1939, feeling badly underpaid, Dandridge left the Negro Leagues to play baseball in Mexico. He remained there for most of the next decade, returning to Newark for a single season (1944). Cleveland Indians owner Bill Veeck reportedly offered Dandridge the chance to join the Cleveland Indians in 1947, but Dandridge turned down the offer.

In 1949 Dandridge returned to the United States to serve as player-manager for the

New York Cubans. That same year, the Cubans sold his rights to the Triple-A Minneapolis Millers, a farm team for the New York Giants. Dandridge shredded the competition. He batted .363 in 1949. Then, in 1950, he led the Millers to a championship while winning the league's MVP award. Yet, inexplicably, the Giants never called up Dandridge. He retired from baseball having never played a big-league game.

Turkey Stearnes

TURKEY STEARNES

While many Negro League stars embraced larger-than-life personalities, center fielder Turkey Stearnes was content to quietly be one of the game's greatest all-around players. Despite some peculiar on-the-field habits—from his awkward, yet effective, batting stance to the fact that he talked to his bats—Stearnes was described as soft-spoken and the type to avoid attention.

Stearnes couldn't help but draw attention as one of the best defensive center fielders in Negro League history. "Cool Papa WAS faster," according to catcher Double Duty Radcliffe. "But Turkey could go get those fly balls better than even Cool Papa. You couldn't hit a ball over his head."

Depending on which story one believes, Norman Thomas Stearnes got the nickname Turkey as a child, either because he had a potbelly or because his running style evoked an image of a flapping turkey. In 1923, at the age of 22, Stearnes made an immediate impact in his first season with the Detroit Stars, batting .362 and slugging 17 home runs.

Stearnes remained with Detroit until 1930 and then bounced from team to team. His most remarkable season may have been 1935 with the Chicago American

THE NAME GAME

It seemed that in the Negro Leagues, every player had a nickname. Cool Papa Bell, Satchel Paige, Cannonball Redding, Copperknee Thompson, King Tut King, and Double Duty Radcliffe were just a few.

Why were there so many interesting nicknames? It may have started in the game's barnstorming days, when entertainment and sideshows were every bit as important as the play between the lines. It continued beyond the barnstorming days, partly because of tradition but also because the players simply spent so much time together. Nicknames were inevitable, and the Negro Leagues were famous for producing some of the most memorable.

Giants. At the age of 34, Stearnes batted an almost ridiculous .430. By then most of his home run power was gone, but he remained an incredible contact hitter and one of the game's best in the field. If not for his reserved personality, Stearnes would have been one of the Negro Leagues' biggest stars. Instead, he remains virtually unknown, a quiet legend known only to true students of the Negro Leagues.

SATCHEL PAIGE

To most modern fans, Satchel Paige was the biggest star of the Negro Leagues. The storied career of the hard-throwing right-hander with unmatched control spanned four decades, with his prime years all coming during baseball's segregation. Paige was a student of the game, a showman and, according to many, including legendary MLB star Joe DiMaggio, the greatest pitcher of his era.

Leroy Robert Page was born July 7, 1906, in Mobile, Alabama. He earned his nickname, Satchel, when he worked as a boy transporting bags at a train station. His family changed the spelling of their last name shortly before Satchel's baseball career got started.

By any name, Paige was a dominant baseball force. After making his Negro League debut in 1926, Paige bounced from team to team—even country to country—always in search of the richest paycheck. Six feet three and lanky, Paige never seemed to tire. Historians believe that during some seasons he pitched more

Satchel Paige thrilled fans with his unique pitching style and unmatched durability.

than 100 games. Most agree that at the pro level, no one in history has thrown more pitches than Paige. And he didn't just throw them. He *named* them. From his bee ball and his trouble ball to his whipsy-dipsy-do, Paige had a style all his own, and the fans loved him for it.

Yet despite the brutal workload, Paige's arm held up. It wasn't until the late 1930s that he started to have arm problems. Some thought his career might be over (one doctor reportedly told him he'd never pitch again). But after slowing down for a season to heal, Paige was back and better than ever.

In the early 1940s, Paige was the star pitcher for the Kansas City Monarchs. His mythic bases-loaded strikeout of Josh Gibson in the 1942 Negro World Series propelled Kansas City to the championship. Paige pitched in all four games as Kansas City swept the Homestead Grays.

In 1948 Paige finally got the chance he'd waited a lifetime for. On July 7, his 42nd birthday, he signed with the Cleveland Indians. Two days later, he became the oldest player ever to make his MLB debut. Paige finished the season 6–1 with a stellar 2.48 ERA. He stayed with the Indians in 1949 and then pitched three seasons for the St. Louis Browns. Paige made a brief return to the big leagues in 1965 to make a single appearance for the Kansas City Athletics. At the age of 59, Paige pitched three innings against the Boston Red Sox. He struck out one batter and didn't give up a run.

Asked about pitching at such an age, Paige—known for his way with words—answered, "How old would you be if you didn't know how old you are?"

Paige was elected to the Hall of Fame in 1971. He died in 1982 at the age of 75.

COUNTLESS STARS

The list of memorable Negro League players goes on and on. Volumes could be written about their stories and personalities.

Fireballing Smokey Joe Williams challenged Satchel Paige as the Negro Leagues' most dominating pitcher. Williams also took his talents into exhibition games against white players, in which he posted a 22–7 record. The most impressive of those wins was a 10-inning no-hitter against the reigning MLB champion New York Giants.

Smokey Joe Williams *(left)* and Dick Redding *(right)*

Another force on the mound was Cannonball Dick Redding. While he didn't enjoy the overall success of Paige or Williams, he may have been the hardest thrower in the Negro Leagues. The nickname Cannonball fit him well.

First baseman Mule Suttles was a big swinger. When he wasn't striking out, he was hitting the ball a long way. Suttles's greatest claim to fame came during winter ball, playing in Havana, Cuba's Tropical Park. The center field fence was 500 feet from home plate and stood 60 feet high. Suttles hit a mammoth home run that cleared it. Then the ball sailed over the heads of soldiers standing beyond the fence.

This 1949 photo of Luke Easter shows the slugger in his San Diego Padres uniform, a Cleveland Indians farm team at the time. From 1950 to 1952, Easter averaged more than 28 home runs and 102 RBI for the Indians.

Suttles and Ray Dandridge were half of the Newark Eagles million-dollar infield. They were joined by shortstop Willie Wells and second baseman Dick Seay. Wells, one of the dominant shortstops of his time, had tremendous range, a reliable glove, and a solid bat, though some criticized the strength of his throwing arm. Seay was peerless with the glove, though he wasn't the threat at the plate that the other three infielders were.

Josh Gibson may have been the best hitting catcher in baseball history. But many believe Biz Mackey was Gibson's superior in the field. A defensive wizard with a rocket for an arm, Mackey earned the respect of his peers. Cool Papa Bell called Mackey, "the best catcher I ever saw."

Luke Easter was a giant of a man, famous for his mammoth moon shot home runs. Easter starred for the Grays in the final days of the Negro Leagues. According to legend, a fan once told Easter that he'd seen Easter's longest home run. Easter replied, "If it came down, it wasn't my longest." Easter, one of the most popular players of the Negro Leagues, went on to play for the Cleveland Indians.

5 THE LEGACY
OF THE NEGRO LEAGUES

It's easy to view the Negro Leagues through the lens of tragedy. They were born of rampant racism and hatred, the result of MLB owners barring talented players from sharing baseball's biggest stage because of their skin color. Yet the Negro Leagues became in many ways a triumph, succeeding and eventually thriving in the face of that racism and hatred. They provided African Americans of the time with a vibrant sports culture that was apart from, yet not inferior to, big-league baseball. At the time, the stars of the Negro Leagues rarely got the acclaim they deserved. But as the social climate in the United States shifted, views on the Negro Leagues have changed.

CHANGING PERCEPTIONS

By the early 1950s, MLB was no longer segregated. But that didn't mean that the battle was over for black ballplayers. For the next several decades, black players still faced abuse and unequal treatment. When Hank Aaron, who played from 1954 to 1976, was chasing down Babe Ruth's career home run record, Aaron was the subject of terrible abuse and even death threats. Yet slowly but surely, stars such as Mays and Aaron were changing white fans' perceptions of black ballplayers.

The civil rights movement really kicked into gear in the 1960s, with minorities demanding—and earning—equal treatment in all aspects of life. The move toward greater equality was reflected on the baseball diamond. In 1962 Buck O'Neil became MLB's first black assistant coach when he signed with the Chicago Cubs. Two years later, the Giants named Willie Mays the first black team captain. In 1966 Emmett Ashford became the first black umpire. Then in 1975, Frank Robinson signed with the Indians as the league's first black manager. Integration finally reached the top of an MLB front office in 1976 when the Atlanta Braves made Bill Lucas the team's general manager. The gains may have come too slowly, but they did come. By the 1980s, baseball's culture of segregation was all but gone.

After leading the Cleveland Indians as MLB's first black manager, Frank Robinson would go on to manage the San Francisco Giants, the Baltimore Orioles, and the Montreal Expos (the Expos moved to Washington, DC, while Robinson was manager).

Meanwhile, the historical view of Negro League players was changing as well. By the late 1960s, baseball's Hall of Fame still had no Negro League stars. In 1966 the legendary Ted Williams was inducted. In his induction speech, Williams called for that to change. "Baseball gives every American boy a chance to excel," Williams said. "Not just to be as good as anybody else, but to be better. This is the nature of man and the name of the game. I hope some day Satchel Paige and Josh Gibson will be voted into the Hall of Fame as symbols of the great Negro players who are not here only because they weren't given the chance."

That wish came true five years later. In 1971 the Hall of Fame created the Negro League Committee to recognize the greats of black baseball. That year the committee selected Satchel Paige as the first Negro League player to be enshrined in the Hall. Gibson and Buck Leonard followed in 1972. By 2001, 22 Negro League players had been enshrined.

Satchel Paige speaks in front of a photo of himself on February 9, 1971, the day he was nominated to the Hall of Fame. He was inducted in August of that year.

BASEBALL'S DIVERSE FUTURE

In recent decades, baseball has become a truly international game. Starting in the mid-1980s, an explosion of Latin American-born talent began to change the face of the game. In 1985 about 11 percent of MLB players were of Latin descent. By 2012 that number had soared to almost 27 percent. The number of players of Asian descent has also been on the rise, climbing from almost none in the early 1990s to about 2 percent by 2010.

Yet while the game has taken on an increasingly multicultural flavor, the number of black players has been on a steady and, to some people, alarming decline. In 1975, 19 percent of MLB players were black. By 2000 that number dropped to 13 percent. And by 2012, it was down to a mere 7.2 percent—figures not seen since the 1950s.

The reasons for this drop in the percentage of black players aren't entirely clear. It may be the result

Black superstars of the modern game, such as Andrew McCutchen of the Pittsburgh Pirates *(top)* and the Chicago Cubs' Jason Heyward *(bottom)*, make up a smaller percentage of MLB players than in recent decades.

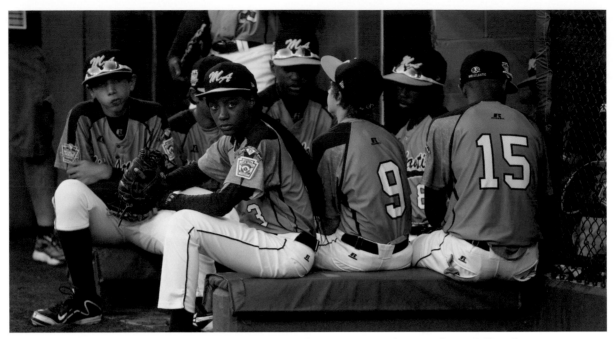

Fewer black athletes are playing baseball than in the past, but African American Mo'ne Davis *(center left)* made news in 2014 as the first girl to pitch a shutout in Little League World Series history.

of a number of factors. Young black athletes may simply be overlooking baseball in favor of other, faster-paced sports—mainly basketball and football. Some have pointed to a lack of baseball facilities in parts of big cities that have large black populations. Others cite the rise in Latin players taking roster spots that may have once gone to black players. Whatever the reasons, the trend seems to be continuing. Major League Baseball has taken steps to remedy the problem, starting programs such as Reviving Baseball in Inner Cities (RBI) to promote baseball among young black athletes.

Not everyone agrees on whether the drop in the percentage of black MLB players is a big problem. Yet one thing is certain. The shape of the modern MLB roster is determined by talent rather than race. While societal factors may encourage black athletes to pursue other sports, they no longer impede those who have the talent to thrive in the big leagues. In that regard, at least, the playing field is level.

Members of the Philadelphia Phillies wear number 42 in honor of Jackie Robinson before a game on April 15, 2016. Each year, all MLB players wear Robinson's number on April 15 to honor the anniversary of his first MLB game.

Yet the legacy of the Negro Leagues continues to resonate in the modern game. Jackie Robinson's jersey number, 42, has been retired by every big-league team. The number stands as a celebration of baseball's integration but also as a reminder of a day when the color of a player's skin mattered more than the quality of his play. And perhaps seeing that number will inspire curiosity and questions among new generations of baseball fans. Those who really want to know the full story of professional baseball will have to look beyond just MLB record books. They'll have to look into the tragedy of a nation's racist history, as well as the triumph of the players who made their mark in spite of it all.

SOURCE NOTES

7   Harold Seymour, *Baseball* (New York: Oxford University Press, 1960), 42.

8–9   Patricia C. McKissack and Frederick McKissack Jr., *Black Diamond: The Story of the Negro Baseball Leagues* (New York: Scholastic, 1994), 28.

11   Robert Peterson, *Only the Ball Was White* (Englewood Cliffs, NJ: Prentice-Hall, 1970), 32.

11   Ibid., 32–33.

13   McKissack and McKissack, *Black Diamond*, 15.

23–24   Lawrence D. Hogan, *Shades of Glory: The Negro Leagues and the Story of African-American Baseball* (Washington, DC: National Geographic Society, 2006), 178.

26   Ibid., 234.

28   Marcus Hayes, "'The Mecca of Black Baseball' in Negro Leagues, the All-Star Game Was Bigger Event Than World Series," *Philly.com*, July 2, 1996, http://articles.philly.com/1996-07-02/sports/25621333_1 _kansas-city-monarchs-east-west-josh-gibson.

28   Ibid.

32–33   Hogan, *Shades of Glory*, 288.

35   Jon Paul Morosi, "Newk: Why It Had to Be Jackie," *FoxSports.com*, April 10, 2013, http://www.foxsports .com/mlb/story/don-newcombe-tells-why-jackie-robinson-was-right-man-to-integrate-major-league -baseball-041013.

40   "Cool Papa Bell," National Baseball Hall of Fame, accessed June 3, 2016, http://baseballhall.org/hof/bell -cool-papa.

41   Hogan, *Shades of Glory*, 245.

42   "Buck Leonard," Baseball-Reference.com, accessed June 3, 2016, http://www.baseball-reference.com /bullpen/Buck_Leonard.

43   "Buck Leonard," National Baseball Hall of Fame, accessed June 3, 2016, http://baseballhall.org/hof /leonard-buck.

43   Larry Schwartz, "No Joshing about Gibson's Talents," *ESPN.com*, accessed June 3, 2016, https://espn .go.com/sportscentury/features/00016050.html.

44   "Josh Gibson," National Baseball Hall of Fame, accessed June 3, 2016, http://baseballhall.org/hof/gibson -josh.

45   Ibid.

45 "Pop Lloyd," National Baseball Hall of Fame, accessed June 3, 2016, http://baseballhall.org/hof/lloyd
-pop.

46 Stew Thornley, "Toni Stone," SABR.org, accessed June 3, 2016, http://sabr.org/bioproj/person/2f33485c.

47 "Oscar Charleston," National Baseball Hall of Fame, accessed June 3, 2016, http://baseballhall.org/hof
/charleston-oscar.

48 "Ray Dandridge," National Baseball Hall of Fame, accessed June 3, 2016, http://baseballhall.org/hof
/dandridge-ray.

49 "On Thanksgiving, Get to Know Hall of Famer Turkey Stearnes," MLB.com, November 26, 2015,
http://m.mlb.com/cutfour/2015/11/26/158219104.

52 Dayn Perry, "Satchel Paige Could Have Been Best Ever," *Foxsports.com*, April 13, 2011, http://www
.foxsports.com/mlb/story/Satchel-Paige-was-greatest-in-Negro-League-and-baseball-pitching-041311.

53 "Biz Mackey," National Baseball Hall of Fame, accessed June 3, 2016, http://baseballhall.org/hof/mackey
-biz.

53 Rick Swaine, *The Black Stars Who Made Baseball Whole: The Jackie Robinson Generation in the Major
Leagues, 1947–1959* (Jefferson, NC: McFarland, 2006), 75.

56 Tom Singer, "Teddy Ballgame Makes Difference for Negro Leaguers to Enter Hall," MLB.com, accessed
June 3, 2016, http://mlb.mlb.com/mlb/history/mlb_negro_leagues_story.jsp?story=williams_ted.

GLOSSARY

barnstorming: the practice of athletes or entertainers traveling from city to city to perform

color barrier: an informal agreement by MLB owners not to sign any black players

contact hitter: a batter who does not strike out often

dynasty: a long period of dominance by one team

exhibition: a game that does not count in any formal standings

integration: the act of joining two or more groups that had previously been separated

Jim Crow law: a state or local law that enforced segregation

segregation: the legal separation of races

slur: insult

FURTHER READING

Books

Doeden, Matt. *The World Series: Baseball's Biggest Stage*. Minneapolis: Millbrook Press, 2014.
Author Matt Doeden takes readers on a journey through the past and present of the greatest championship in sports.

Nelson, Kadir. *We Are the Ship: The Story of Negro League Baseball*. New York: Jump at the Sun, 2008.
Learn more about the Negro Leagues in this beautifully illustrated book.

Panchyk, Richard. *Baseball History for Kids: America at Bat from 1900 to Today with 19 Activities*. Chicago: Chicago Review Press, 2016.
This book details the history of America's Pastime, including the Negro Leagues.

Smith, Charles R., Jr. *Stars in the Shadows: The Negro League All-Star Game of 1934*. New York: Atheneum, 2012.
This illustrated book will make you feel as if you're at the 1934 East-West Classic, a game considered one of the best ever by many baseball historians.

Websites

ESPN—Black History Month
http://espn.go.com/espn/feature/index?page=blackhistory
ESPN's website honoring the contributions of African American athletes has a lot of interesting information about the Negro Leagues.

MLB—Negro Leagues Legacy
http://mlb.mlb.com/mlb/history/mlb_negro_leagues.jsp
MLB's Negro Leagues website has enough photos, fascinating facts, and special features to keep any baseball historian busy.

National Baseball Hall of Fame
http://baseballhall.org
Visit the official website of the Hall of Fame to learn all about baseball heroes from the Negro Leagues to the newly inducted class of 2016.

Negro Leagues Baseball Museum
https://www.nlbm.com
Check out the official website of the Negro Leagues Baseball Museum and plan a trip to visit the museum in Kansas City, Missouri.

INDEX

ABOUT THE AUTHOR

Matt Doeden began his career as a sportswriter, covering everything from high school sports to the NFL. Since then he has written hundreds of children's and young adult books on topics ranging from history to sports to current events. His titles *Sandy Koufax, Tom Brady: Unlikely Champion, The College Football Championship: The Fight for the Top Spot, The World Series: Baseball's Biggest Stage,* and *The Final Four: The Pursuit of College Basketball Glory* were Junior Library Guild selections. His title *Darkness Everywhere: The Assassination of Mohandas Gandhi* was listed among the Best Children's Books of the Year by the Children's Book Committee at Bank Street College. Doeden, an avid baseball fan, lives in Minnesota with his wife and two children.

PHOTO ACKNOWLEDGMENTS

The images in this book are used with the permission of: © iStockphoto.com/ginosphotos, p. 1; © iStockphoto.com/gmcoop (baseball background throughout); © Transcendental Graphics/Getty Images, pp. 4, 12, 13, 18, 20, 21, 22 (left), 22 (right), 31, 33, 43, 46, 48; National Baseball Hall of Fame Library, Cooperstown, N.Y., pp. 6, 22 (middle), 26, 28, 30, 40, 41, 42, 47, 49, 51, 52; The Miriam and Ira D. Wallach Division of Art, Prints and Photographs, The New York Public Library, Astor, Lenox and Tilden Foundations, p. 9; © Diamond Images/Getty Images, pp. 14, 45; Library of Congress (LC-B2-4992-4), p. 15; © Chicago History Museum/Getty Images, p. 17; Picture History/Newscom, p. 23; Library of Congress (LC-DIG-ppmsca-18576), p. 24; © Iconic Archive/Getty Images, p. 25; © Teenie Harris Archive/Carnegie Museum of Art/Getty Images, p. 27; AP Photo, pp. 29, 34, 37; © Everett Collection Inc/Alamy, p. 35; AP Photo/John Rooney, p. 36; AP Photo/David F. Smith, p. 53; © Tony Tomsic/Getty Images, p. 55; Everett Collection/Newscom, p. 56; Scott W. Grau/Icon Sportswire CBW/Newscom, p. 57 (top); Chris Lee/TNS/Newscom, p. 57 (bottom); AP Photo/Gene J. Puskar, p. 58; © Rich Schultz/Getty Images, p. 59.

Cover photo and jacket flap: © Bettmann/Getty Images.